taking tea at the Savoy

Anton Edelmann

PAVILION

First published in Great Britain in 1999 by
PAVILION BOOKS
64 Brewery Road, London, N7 9NT

A member of **Chrysalis** Books plc

This paperback edition first published in
Great Britain in 2002 by
Pavilion Books

Photographs by Laurie Evans

Designed by Andrew Barron &
Collis Clements Associates

Typeset in Bembo & Goudy Sans

A CIP catalogue record for this book is
available from the British Library.

ISBN 1 86205 631 5

Colour reproduction by Anglia Graphics, UK.
Printed and bound in Italy by Giunti,
Prato

10 9 8 7 6 5 4 3 2 1

This book may be ordered direct from the
publisher. Please contact the Marketing
Department. But try your bookshop first.

ACKNOWLEDGEMENTS
Nothing good is ever achieved without
enthusiasm. For showing that essential
quality in abundance, and for their
dedication and hard work, I thank all the
colleagues and friends who helped me
with this book. My special thanks to the
Managing Director of the Savoy Group, Mr
Pajares, the General Manager of the Savoy,
Mr Shepherd, and the Food and Beverage
Manager, Mr Krenzer, for their help and
generosity. My thanks and gratitude to
the chefs in the Savoy Restaurant kitchen,
especially the Head Pastry Chef, William
Curley, Derek Rook, Stephen Will, Paul
Hart, Nicholas Duncan and all the others
who showed so much patience,
understanding and goodwill.

BIBLIOGRAPHY

A Cup of Tea by Geraldene Holt
(Pavilion, 1991)

That Tea Book by Patricia Rose Cress
(1990)

The Book of Tea & Coffee by Sarah Jane
Evans and Giles Hilton (Pavilion, 1998)

The East India Company Book of Tea by
Antony Wild (HarperCollins, 1997)

The New Penguin Dictionary of
Quotations by JM and MJ Cohen
(Penguin, 1996)

The Penguin Dictionary of Twentieth-
Century Quotations by JM and MJ Cohen
(Penguin, 1996)

contents

ALFRESCO TEA

Cheese Puffs with Guacamole

Tomato Snails

Lemon Feuilletés

Pear Custard Tarts

Cinnamon Madeleines

Exotic Fruit Tartlets

Baked Chocolate Cheesecake

Pineapple and Ginger Cakes

Cheese Sablés

TRADITIONAL TEA

Prawn and Spring Onion Sandwiches
with Sun-dried Tomato Bread

Creamed Avocado Sandwiches with
Plum Tomato and Red Onion

Scones

Strawberry Tartlets

Savoy Choux Pastry Swans

Traditional French Orange Tart

Dundee Cake

CHILDREN'S AFTERNOON TEA

Honey and Ham Biscuits

Royal Biscuits

Doughnuts

Apricot and Pecan Sticky Buns

Hot Chocolate Pudding

CELEBRATORY TEA

Herb Scones with White Crab Meat
and Keta Caviar

Mini Meringues

Light and Simple Fruit Cake

Cherry Tart with Streusel

Raspberry Mille-feuilles

introduction

Think of afternoon tea and what comes to mind? Ladies in smart hats, floral tea dresses and white gloves, sipping Earl Grey from bone china cups, little finger poised in mid-air, then daintily cutting off a piece of fruit tart with a silver cake fork or delicately eating a cucumber sandwich, crusts removed, while a pianist tinkles in the background and the murmur of polite conversation fills the air.

This image isn't far from the modern-day reality at The Savoy – except that there are no hats or gloves in sight. On a typical afternoon, the room is filled with couples young and old, Japanese tourists (a nation that truly understands the ritualistic tea ceremony) and a daughter treating her elderly mother to tea, while the waiters hover, all smiles and charm, ready to replenish a flagging teapot or check that all is perfection. A popular venue for royalty, heads of state and celebrities, recent sightings at The Savoy include film stars, supermodels, pop stars and countless other celebrities.

'There are few hours in life more agreeable than the hour dedicated to the ceremony known as afternoon tea.'

The Portrait of a Lady,
Henry James

Quintessentially British, utterly civilised and a treat that should be enjoyed on a regular basis, there is nothing quite like afternoon tea – and The Savoy serves 800 a week, in the elegant and luxurious Thames Foyer. Green and pink predominate, from the bucket chairs to carpet and table linen. The tea itself is served on white china with a pink candy stripe border decorated with a large scroll-like S. A dinner-jacketed pianist plays a white grand piano, decorated with black silhouettes of flappers, biplanes and bellboys bearing trays of cocktails; murals of pastoral scenes and art deco mirrors that are a testament to kitsch add to the feeling of luxurious wellbeing.

Patricia Rose Cress writes in *That Tea Book*, 'It is a near-perfect setting, a trompe l'oeil garden surrounds you, complemented by beautiful Art Deco mirrors. Settle down in a comfortable sofa and wonder at the unparalleled ambience'.

It is, above all, a place to linger. What better setting for a good gossip with a girlfriend, a birthday treat with the family, a spot of indulgence on a rainy afternoon or simply a chance to watch the world go by…

chocolate gâteau with grand marnier

*Makes a 17.5 cm/
7 inch gâteau*

1 sponge cake, 17.5 cm/7 inches in diameter

2 tbsp apricot jam, sieved

125 ml/4 fl oz/½ cup orange juice

5 tbsp Grand Marnier

2 leaves gelatine

350 g/12 oz good-quality milk chocolate

300 ml/10 fl oz/1¼ cups double cream (heavy cream)

1 tbsp ground hazelnuts

For the shortbread base

70 g/scant 2½ oz/½ cup plain flour (all-purpose flour)

30 g/1 oz/2½ tbsp caster sugar (US granulated sugar)

40 g/scant 1½ oz/3 tbsp unsalted butter, at room temperature

1 egg yolk

Heat the oven to 180°C/350°F/gas mark 4. Line a baking sheet with baking parchment.

First make the shortbread base. Combine the flour, sugar and butter in a bowl and rub together to a fine crumb. Bind to a dough with the egg yolk. Put the dough on the paper-lined baking sheet and press it out to a neat round about 5 mm/ ¼ inch thick and 17.5 cm/7 inches in diameter. Prick the surface all over with a fork. Chill for 15 minutes.

Bake the shortbread round for about 12 minutes or until golden brown. Leave to cool on a wire rack.

Cut a 5 mm/¼ inch thick layer from the sponge cake and reserve. Keep the remainder of the cake for another recipe.

Line a cold baking sheet with baking parchment. Put the shortbread base on the parchment. Warm the apricot jam until melted. Spread the jam evenly over the shortbread. Set the sponge cake layer on top and press gently together. Line the sides of an 18.5 cm/7½ inch flan ring that is 5 cm/2 inches deep with baking parchment. Place it on the baking sheet and place the shortbread and cake inside.

Mix half of the orange juice with 1½ tbsp of the Grand Marnier. Using a pastry brush, moisten the cake with the mixture.

Soak the gelatine leaves in 3½ tbsp cold water until softened. Drain the gelatine and squeeze out excess water, then return to the bowl. Add the remaining orange juice and Grand Marnier. Set the bowl in a pan of simmering water and stir to melt the gelatine. Do not let the mixture boil.

Break the chocolate into a heatproof bowl or into the top of a double boiler. Set over a pan of simmering water and stir the chocolate until it is melted and smooth. Remove from the heat and cool slightly. Add the gelatine mixture.

Whip the cream until thick but not stiff. Add the chocolate mixture and stir to a smooth, velvety consistency. Pour the chocolate mixture slowly around the rim of the cake, inside the flan ring, so it runs down the sides into the gap between the cake and the flan ring, then pour on to the centre of the cake and smooth the top. Put the hazelnuts in a coarse sieve and rub through to dust the surface of the chocolate cream.

Cover and chill for about 1½ hours or until the chocolate cream has set.

carrot cake with almonds

*Makes a 20 cm/
8 inch cake*

120 g/4 oz/1⅓ cups stale white breadcrumbs

3 eggs, separated

1 egg yolk

120 g/4 oz/½ cup + 2 tbsp caster sugar (US granulated sugar)

¼ tsp pure vanilla extract

finely grated zest of ½ lemon

1 tbsp lemon juice

150 g/5 oz/1⅓ cups carrots, peeled and finely grated

90 g/3 oz/1¼ cups ground almonds

30 g/1 oz/¼ cup blanched almonds, roughly chopped

½ tsp baking powder

¼ tsp ground allspice

pinch of salt

¼ tsp cream of tartar

icing sugar to dust

Heat the oven to 200°C/400°F/gas mark 6.

Butter a 20 cm/8 inch round cake tin and coat with some of the breadcrumbs. Beat the 4 egg yolks, sugar, vanilla extract, and lemon zest and juice in an electric mixer until the mixture looks slightly pale and is thick enough to coat the back of a spoon.

Mix the grated carrots and all the almonds with the remaining breadcrumbs, the baking powder, allspice and salt. Fold into the egg yolk mixture with a spoon.

Whisk the egg whites with the cream of tartar until they form soft peaks. Fold them gently but thoroughly into the carrot mixture. Transfer to the prepared cake tin and bake for 30–40 minutes or until risen and firm to the touch. Turn out on to a wire rack to cool.

Dust with icing sugar before serving.

cinnamon madeleines

Makes 15

These small shell-shaped cakes were created in France in the seventeenth century by Madeleine Simonin, who was the personal cook of Jean-Paul de Gondi, Cardinal de Retz. Madeleine devised the recipe in the kitchens of the Cardinal's residence in the city of Commercy, in north-eastern France. He was so delighted with the little cakes that he christened them madeleines.

3 eggs

185 g/6½ oz/¾ cup + 3 tbsp caster sugar (US granulated sugar)

250 g/8½ oz/1¼ cups plain flour (all-purpose flour)

2½ tsp baking powder

1¼ tsp ground cinnamon

70 ml/2½ fl oz/5 tbsp milk

125 g/4½ oz/9 tbsp unsalted butter, melted to blood temperature

Beat together the eggs and sugar until creamy. Sift the flour, baking powder and cinnamon into the bowl and add the milk. Mix until smooth. Add the butter and beat until homogenous. Rest in the refrigerator for 20 minutes.

Heat the oven to 190°C/375°F/gas mark 5.

Pipe the mixture into greased and floured shell-shaped madeleine moulds. Alternatively you can use 5 cm/2 inch paper baking cases. Bake for 6 minutes.

Remove from the moulds immediately and cool on a wire rack.

mini meringues

Makes 12

80 g/2¾ oz/5 tbsp egg whites

160 g/5½ oz/¾ cup caster sugar
(superfine sugar)

100 ml/3½ fl oz/½ cup double cream
(heavy cream), whipped

Heat the oven to 110°C/225°F/gas
mark ¼. Line a baking tray with
baking parchment.

In a heatproof bowl set over a pan of
hot water, whisk the egg whites and
sugar together until the sugar
dissolves. Remove from the heat and
whisk with an electric mixer until
the volume is doubled and you have
a stiff meringue.

Spoon the meringue into a piping
bag fitted with a plain nozzle.
Pipe cylindrical shapes on to the
parchment, making them about
3 cm/1¼ inches wide at the base and
3 cm/1¼ inches high. You should
have 24 mini meringues. Dry out in
the oven for 4 hours.

To serve, spread a small amount of
whipped cream on to the base of the
meringues and press them lightly
together in pairs.

dundee cake

Makes a 15 cm/
6 inch cake

The town of Dundee in the east of Scotland is famous for not one but two local specialities, Dundee cake and Dundee marmalade. The world-renowned Dundee marmalade was created by a local grocer, and at the beginning of the eighteenth century the first marmalade factory was built in Dundee in order to produce the famous preserve on a commercial basis.

The commercial production of the marmalade resulted in a by-product of orange peel. This is where Scottish ingenuity comes into force. Instead of wasting the surplus orange peel, the canny Scots created the recipe for Dundee cake, using the orange peel as flavouring, giving this cake its distinctive and unique taste.

125 g/4¼ oz/8½ tbsp unsalted butter, at room temperature

185 g/6 oz/¾ cup + 3 tbsp caster sugar (US granulated sugar)

2 large eggs

185 g/6 oz/1⅓ cups plain flour (all-purpose flour)

1 tsp baking powder

200 g/7 oz/1⅓ cups sultanas (golden raisins)

150 g/5 oz/1 cup candied orange peel, cut into fine strips

grated zest of ½ orange

grated zest of ½ lemon

30 g/1 oz/¼ cup whole blanched almonds

caster sugar (US granulated sugar) to sprinkle

Heat the oven to 180°C/350°F/gas mark 4. Grease and flour a deep 15 cm/6 inch cake tin.

Cream together the butter and sugar until light and creamy. Slowly add the eggs, ensuring the mixture does not split. Sift in the flour and baking powder, and fold in, then mix in the sultanas, orange peel, and orange and lemon zest.

Spoon into the prepared tin, filling it three-quarters full. Flatten the top of the cake with the back of your wet hand. Arrange the blanched almonds evenly around the edge of the cake, lightly pressing them in.

Bake for 45–50 minutes. To test whether the cake is cooked, insert a small knife into the centre; it should come out clean.

Leave to cool in the tin. Before serving, sprinkle the top with caster sugar.

light and simple fruit cake

*Makes a
large loaf cake*

150 g/5 oz/10 tbsp unsalted butter,
at room temperature

125 g/4½ oz/¼ cup demerara sugar

4 large eggs (US extra large eggs),
lightly beaten

200 g/7 oz/1⅓ cups plain flour
(all-purpose flour)

4 tsp baking powder

1 tsp ground cinnamon

1 tsp mixed spice (apple pie spice)

45 g/1½ oz/heaped ⅓ cup walnut
pieces, coarsely chopped

90 g/3 oz/½ cup glacé cherries
(candied cherries), cut in half

75 g/2½ oz/½ cup candied orange
peel, diced

75 g/2½ oz/½ cup candied lemon
peel, diced

30 g/1 oz/2 tbsp candied angelica,
diced

150 g/5 oz/1 cup raisins

Heat the oven to 170°C/325°F/gas
mark 3. Grease a 900 g/2 1b loaf tin
that measures about 23 x 12.5 x
7.5 cm/9 x 5 x 3 inches, then line it
with greaseproof paper (wax paper).

With an electric mixer at high speed,
cream the butter with the sugar
until pale and fluffy. Gradually beat
half of the eggs into the creamed
mixture at medium speed. Sift
together the flour, baking powder
and spices. Add half to the creamed
mixture, then beat in the remaining
eggs followed by the remaining flour.

Add the walnuts, cherries, candied
peel, angelica and raisins to the cake
mixture, and fold them in gently and
evenly. Pour the mixture into the
prepared loaf tin.

Bake for 1–1¼ hours or until the
cake is lightly browned on top and a
skewer inserted into the centre
comes out clean. If the surface is
browning too much towards the end
of baking, cover the cake with foil.

Leave to cool in the tin.

the cup that cheers

'If you are cold, tea will warm you; if you are too heated, it will cool you; if you are depressed, it will cheer you; if you are exhausted, it will calm you.'

William Gladstone

But what is the best way to make our national drink? Although many people have their own idiosyncracies, it is generally agreed that you need to:

★ fill the kettle with freshly drawn cold water – let the tap run a little first.

★ just before the kettle has boiled, warm the pot so that the brewing temperature is correct.

★ discard the water and add 1 heaped teaspoon tea to the pot per person, plus one extra.

★ pour on water as it boils. Over-boiled water is less oxygenated so gives a 'flatter' cup, while already boiled water will not be hot enough.

★ leave it to brew for 5 minutes.

Some people also swear by serving it in a pretty bone china cup – at The Savoy, afternoon tea is taken from one of eight china patterns made exclusively to the hotel's own design.

And, of course, tea must not be over-brewed so that tannin pre-dominates. As Nancy Reagan so memorably said in 1981: 'A woman is like a teabag. It's only when she's in hot water that you realize how strong she is.'

Nor should it be so weak as to be indistinguishable from coffee: 'Look here, Steward, if this is coffee, I want tea; but if this is tea, then I wish for coffee,' summed this taste dilemma up perfectly in a Punch magazine cartoon of 1902; while Jonathan Swift described weak tea as 'no more than water bewitched'.

Anton Edelmann says: 'For a successful afternoon tea you need the right ambience and setting. At The Savoy we have got it right. There are lots of people, so it isn't too hushed. I quite like a bit of life – you are there to watch, aren't you? It's like my grandmother: she didn't 'go out to Kaffee und Kuchen *(the equivalent of afternoon tea in Germany) for the cake – although she liked that as well – she put on a nice hat and went to show it off. That's what it's all about.'*

passionfruit and chocolate shortcake

Serves 16

250 g/8½ oz/1 cup + 2 tbsp
unsalted butter, at room temperature

150 g/5 oz/¾ cup caster sugar
(US granulated sugar)

1 egg

1½ egg yolks

450 g/1 lb/3 cups plain flour
(all-purpose flour), sifted

1 egg, lightly beaten, for the egg
wash

For the filling

90 g/3 oz/½ cup passionfruit pulp

80 g/scant 3 oz/6½ tbsp sugar

4 tbsp crème fraîche

175 g/6 oz milk chocolate

35 g/1¼ oz/2½ tbsp unsalted butter

Mix the butter with the sugar,
beating together well. Add the egg
and egg yolk slowly, then add the
flour and mix to make a smooth
dough. Cover and rest for 2 hours in
the refrigerator.

Put the passionfruit pulp, sugar and
crème fraîche in a saucepan and
bring to the boil, stirring to dissolve
the sugar. Remove from the heat and
cool slightly, then add the chocolate
and butter and stir until smooth.
Pour the mixture into 16 paper cups
that are 5 cm/2 inches in diameter
to make a layer 1 cm/⅓ inches thick.
Allow to set in the refrigerator.

Roll out the dough to 3 mm/⅛ inch
thick and stamp out 7 cm/2¾ inch
rounds with a cutter. Brush them
with beaten egg, then place on a
greased baking tray. Rest in the
fridge for 20 minutes.

Heat the oven to 180°C/350°F/gas
mark 4.

Bake the shortcake rounds for 7–10
minutes or until lightly golden.
Transfer to a wire rack to cool.

Remove the discs of filling from the
paper cups. Top half of the shortcake
rounds with a disc of filling and
place another shortcake round on
this, pressing down lightly.

macaroons

Makes about 36

Macaroons originated in Venice in the thirteenth century. The Venetians christened the small almond cakes '*macerone*' which was the Venetian spelling of the Italian word *maccherone*, meaning a fine paste. The English word macaroon is a derivative of the French word *macaron*.

A creation of the twentieth century are the renowned Macarons Ladurée, which were created by a young French pâtissier named Paul Desfontaines. Whilst working in Switzerland, in a small pâtisserie in Lausanne, he was greatly impressed by a biscuit-based gâteau with a ganache filling. On his return to France he started working for his uncle, Jean Ladurée, who had opened a small pâtisserie. Paul adapted the gâteau recipe to use individual macaroons instead of the biscuit base, sandwiching them together with a variety of flavoured ganaches. He named his new creation Macarons Ladurée, in honour of his uncle. They were an instant success.

125 g/4½ oz/1⅔ cups ground almonds

125 g/4½ oz/1 cup icing sugar (confectioners' sugar)

100 ml/3½ fl oz/scant ½ cup egg whites

1 tsp pure vanilla extract

125 g/4½ oz/½ cup + 2 tbsp caster sugar (US granulated sugar)

100 g/3½ oz/⅓ cup orange marmalade

(Continued on page 26)

Heat the oven to 170°C/325°F/gas mark 3.

Sift the almonds and icing sugar into a bowl. Add half of the egg whites and the vanilla extract, and mix to a smooth paste.

Combine the remaining egg whites with the caster sugar in a heatproof bowl. Warm over a pan of hot water, stirring constantly, until the sugar has dissolved. Remove from the hot water, and beat with an electric mixer to a stiff meringue. Add the almond paste, stirring gently but thoroughly.

Pipe the mixture in blobs about 5 cm/2 inches wide on a baking tray lined with greaseproof paper or baking parchment. Allow a skin to form (about 5 minutes).

Bake for 5–7 minutes. Turn the tray during baking in order to obtain evenly coloured macaroons. Transfer to a wire rack to cool.

When cooled, sandwich together pairs of macaroons with orange marmalade.

For orange macaroons
Add 5 g/½ oz orange essence in place of the vanilla extract.

For pistachio macaroons
Add 20 g/⅔ oz of pistachio paste in place of the vanilla extract.

s a c h e r   t o r t e

Makes a 23 cm/
9 inch cake

140 g/4½ oz/9½ tbsp unsalted butter, softened

100 g/3½ oz/¾ cup + 1 tbsp icing sugar (confectioners' sugar), sifted

1 vanilla pod (vanilla bean), split and seeds scraped out

6 eggs, separated

120 g/4 oz good-quality plain chocolate (semisweet chocolate), melted

120 g/4 oz/¾ cup + 2 tbsp plain flour (all-purpose flour), sifted

100 g/3½ oz/½ cup caster sugar (US granulated sugar)

300 g/10 oz/1 cup orange marmalade, warmed and sieved

a little melted chocolate to decorate (optional)

For the chocolate glaze

5 tbsp milk

4 tbsp double cream (heavy cream)

5 tbsp Sugar Syrup (see page 92)

4 tsp liquid glucose or light corn syrup

300 g/10 oz good-quality plain chocolate (semisweet chocolate), chopped

Heat to the oven to 170°C/325°F/gas mark 3. Grease and line a 23 cm/ 9 inch round cake tin.

Beat the butter and icing sugar together with the vanilla seeds until pale, then beat in the egg yolks one at a time. Fold in the cooled melted chocolate and then the flour until evenly combined.

In a separate bowl, whisk the egg whites until they form soft peaks, then whisk in the caster sugar a spoonful at a time until the mixture is stiff and glossy. Add a large spoonful to the chocolate mixture and fold in completely, then pour the chocolate mixture into the remaining egg whites and fold together gently but thoroughly.

Transfer the mixture to the prepared tin and level the surface. Bake for about 45 minutes or until risen and just firm to the touch. Test by inserting a fine skewer into the centre of the cake; it will come out clean when the cake is cooked. Leave in the tin until cool enough to handle, then turn out on to a wire rack and leave to cool completely.

Cut the cake in half horizontally, then sandwich it back together with about half of the marmalade. Use the rest to cover the top and sides of the cake.

For the glaze, place the milk, cream, sugar syrup and glucose in a saucepan and bring to the boil. Remove from the heat and add the chocolate. Stir until melted and smooth. Allow to cool slightly.

Place the cake on a wire rack set over a tray, and spread the chocolate glaze quickly all over the top and sides with a palette knife (metal spatula). Leave in a cool place to set. If wished, pipe 'Sacher' in melted chocolate on top of the cake.

lemon feuilletés

Makes 40

2 eggs

50 g/1¾ oz/¼ cup caster sugar
(US granulated sugar)

40 g/1½ oz/4½ tbsp plain flour
(all-purpose flour), sifted

For the topping

2 eggs

I egg yolk

125 g/4¼ oz/½ cup + 2 tbsp caster
sugar (US granulated sugar)

finely grated zest of 2 lemons

120 ml/4 fl oz/½ cup fresh lemon
juice, strained

100 g/3½ oz/7 tbsp unsalted butter

2 tsp powdered unflavoured gelatine

2 tbsp dry white wine

100 g/3½ oz luxury plain chocolate
(semisweet or bittersweet chocolate)

Heat the oven to 220°C/425°F/gas
mark 7. Lightly grease a 33 x 23 cm/
13 x 9 inch Swiss roll tin (jelly roll
pan) and line with greaseproof paper
or baking parchment.

Using an electric mixer, whisk the
eggs with the sugar until the
mixture is thick and pale. A clear
trail should be left on the surface of
the mixture when the beaters are
lifted out. Fold in the flour. Transfer
the mixture to the prepared tin and
level the surface. Bake for about
10 minutes or until risen and firm to
the touch. Cool on a wire rack, then
peel off the lining paper.

For the topping, whisk the eggs, egg
yolk, sugar, and lemon zest and juice
together in the top of a double
boiler or a basin. Set over simmering
water and cook for 35–40 minutes or
until thickened, stirring frequently.

Melt 65 g/2 oz/4 tbsp of the butter and stir into the lemon mixture.

Dissolve the gelatine in the white wine over a gentle heat. Stir in a little of the lemon mixture, then add to the rest of the lemon mixture, stirring well.

Trim the crusty edges from the sponge. Lightly oil the tin used for baking the sponge, then set the sponge back in it. Spoon the lemon mixture on top and level the surface. Chill for about 4 hours or until set.

Melt the chocolate with the remaining butter, stirring well until smooth. Spread over the lemon mixture and chill until set.

Cut into very neat squares about 4 x 4 cm/1½ x 1½ inches.

'What makes tea at The Savoy special is the atmosphere in the foyer, being in the centre of the hotel. And we have one of the best pianists in London.'

apple tarts

Makes 6

8 Bramley's or other cooking apples

35 g/1¼ oz/2½ tbsp unsalted butter, melted

45 g/1½ oz/3½ tbsp caster sugar (US granulated sugar)

½ vanilla pod (vanilla bean), split

300 g/10½ oz Sweet Pastry (see page 92)

3 tbsp apricot jam

Peel, core and chop half of the apples. Put into a saucepan with the butter, sugar and vanilla pod. Cook gently until soft. Remove from the heat and cool, then remove the vanilla pod.

Roll out the pastry to 3 mm/⅛ inch thick and line six 7.5 cm/3 inch tartlet moulds. Allow to rest in the refrigerator for 20 minutes.

Heat the oven to 180°C/350°F/gas mark 4.

Line the tart cases with greaseproof paper or baking parchment and fill with baking beans. Bake blind for 15 minutes. Remove the paper and beans, and bake for a further 4 minutes or until golden.

Fill the tart cases with the apple compote. Peel and core the remaining apples, then cut into 2 cm/¾ inch slices. Arrange on top of the apple compote, so the filling is 2–3 cm/about 1 inch higher than the edge of the tart case.

Increase the oven heat to 220°C/425°F/gas mark 7, and bake the tarts for 15–20 minutes. Cool on a wire rack.

Warm the apricot jam until melted, then brush over the apple slices to glaze.

baked chocolate cheesecake

*Makes a 20 cm/
8 inch cheesecake*

250 g/8½ oz Sweet Pastry
(see page 92)

200 g/7 oz/1 cup quark or cream
cheese

3 tbsp unsweetened cocoa powder

60 g/2 oz/5 tbsp caster sugar
(US granulated sugar)

1 egg

150 ml/5 fl oz/⅔ cup double cream
(heavy cream)

75 g/2½ oz good-quality plain
chocolate (semisweet chocolate),
melted

finely grated zest of ½ orange

On a lightly floured surface, roll out
the pastry and use to line a deep
20 cm/8 inch flan tin. Line with
greaseproof paper or baking
parchment, fill with baking beans
and chill for 20 minutes.

Heat the oven to 200°C/400°F/gas
mark 6.

Bake the pastry case for 10 minutes,
then remove the paper and baking
beans. Bake for 10 minutes longer.
Leave to cool. Reduce the oven
temperature to 180°C/350°F/gas
mark 4.

Beat the cheese with the cocoa
powder, sugar and egg until smooth,
then stir in the cream. Fold in the
cooled melted chocolate and the
orange zest. Transfer to the pastry
case. Bake for about 20 minutes or
until just set, then leave to cool.

bakewell tart

*Makes a
20 cm/8 inch tart*

250 g/8½ oz Sweet Pastry
(see page 92)

2 tbsp raspberry jam

400 g/14 oz Frangipane
(see page 90)

60 g/2 oz/⅔ cup flaked almonds
(sliced almonds)

100 g/3½ oz/¾ cup icing sugar
(confectioners' sugar)

2 tsp Kirsch liqueur

½ tsp lemon juice

3 tbsp apricot jam

Roll out the pastry to 5 mm/¼ inch
thick and line a 20 cm/8 inch flan
ring set on a baking sheet. Allow to
rest for 20 minutes in the
refrigerator.

Heat the oven to 170°C/325°F/gas
mark 3.

Spread a thin layer of raspberry jam
on the bottom of the tart case. Fill
the tart just three-quarters full with
the frangipane. Sprinkle the top with
the flaked almonds.

Bake for 35–40 minutes. Remove
from the oven and leave to cool.

Mix the icing sugar, Kirsch and
lemon juice to a smooth paste in a
small saucepan, and heat gently.
Carefully spread the mixture in a
thin layer on top of the tart and
allow to set.

Heat the apricot jam until melted
and brush a thin layer over the top.

exotic fruit tartlets

Makes 4

100 g/3½ oz Puff Pastry
(see page 91)

½ quantity Frangipane
(see page 90)

1 tbsp passionfruit juice, strained

4 tbsp Pastry Cream (see page 88) or
whipped cream

½ kiwi fruit, peeled and sliced

¼ mango, peeled, stoned and sliced

¼ small pineapple, peeled, cored and
sliced

¼ pawpaw or papaya, peeled, seeded
and sliced

4 tbsp apricot jam, warmed and
sieved, to glaze

4 tiny sprigs of fresh mint

On a lightly floured surface, roll out
the pastry thinly and use to line four
7.5 cm/3 inch tartlet tins. Leave to
rest in a cool place for 15 minutes.

Heat the oven to 200°C/400°F/gas
mark 6.

Divide the frangipane among the
pastry cases and bake for 10–15
minutes or until golden brown.
Leave to cool.

Stir the passionfruit juice into the
pastry cream or whipped cream and
spoon it into the tartlets. Arrange
the fruit on top. Brush with apricot
jam, then decorate with the mint
sprigs.

cherry tart with streusel

Serves 6

125 ml/4 fl oz/½ cup milk

15 g/½ oz/1 cake fresh yeast

3 tbsp vegetable oil

250 g/9 oz/2 cups strong white flour
(hard flour)

2 tsp caster sugar
(US granulated sugar)

1 tsp salt

250 g/9 oz Frangipane
(see page 90)

900 g/2 lb ripe cherries, stones
removed

For the streusel

120 g/4 oz/¾ cup + 2 tbsp plain
flour (all-purpose flour)

3 tbsp caster sugar
(US granulated sugar)

1 tsp ground allspice

90 g/3 oz/6 tbsp cold unsalted
butter

Warm the milk to lukewarm and
pour it into a large bowl. Add the
yeast and mash with a spoon until
creamy. Stir in the oil. Leave in a
warm place for 10 minutes.

Sift the flour, sugar and salt into the
bowl and mix to make a smooth
dough. Turn out on to a lightly
floured surface and knead for 8–10
minutes or until smooth and elastic.
Put the dough into an oiled bowl,
cover with oiled cling film (plastic
wrap) and leave to rise in a warm
place for 40 minutes or until doubled
in bulk.

Butter a 23 x 33 cm/9 x 13 inch Swiss roll tin (jelly roll pan). Knead the dough lightly, then, on a floured surface, roll it out to a rectangle. Put it in the centre of the buttered tin and press it out to line the bottom and sides. Spread the frangipane over the bottom of the dough case. Chill for 20 minutes.

Heat the oven to 180°C/350°F/gas mark 4.

For the streusel, combine the flour, sugar and allspice in a bowl. Cut the butter into small cubes and rub into the dry ingredients until the mixture resembles large pea-size crumbs.

Arrange the cherries lightly on top of the frangipane. Sprinkle the streusel evenly over the top. Bake for about 55 minutes or until the tart base and the streusel topping are golden brown. Serve warm, cut into squares.

As Alice Walker remarks in The Color Purple:*'Tea to the English is really a picnic indoors.'*

mini choux buns

Makes 10

1 quantity Choux Pastry
(see page 90)

20 g/¾ oz/1 tbsp instant coffee,
dissolved in a little water

1 quantity Pastry Cream
(see page 88)

200 g/7 oz fondant

1 tbsp Sugar Syrup (see page 92)

Heat the oven to 200°C/400°F/gas
mark 6. Line a baking tray with
greaseproof paper or baking
parchment.

Using a 1 cm/½ inch plain nozzle,
pipe the choux paste on to the
paper-lined tray, in 10 blobs
2.5 cm/1 inch in diameter and 10

that are 5 cm/2 inches in diameter.
Bake for 12 minutes, then reduce the
heat to 180°C/350°F/gas mark 4 and
bake for a further 10 minutes.
Remove and cool.

Stir half of the coffee into the pastry
cream. Pierce a small hole in each of
the choux buns and pipe in the
pastry cream, ensuring that each
bun is filled.

Mix together the fondant, sugar
syrup and remaining coffee in a
saucepan and heat gently to
37°C/98.6°F (blood temperature).
Do not heat above this or the
fondant will lose its shine.

Dip the top of each bun into the
fondant, and place a small bun on
top of a large one.

reading the tea leaves

Thomas De Quincey's 'favoured beverage of the intellectual', tea comes in a wide variety of leaves and flavours. Darjeeling, Assam, Earl Grey... if you're not already a tea aficionado, the choice on offer can seem bewildering. At The Savoy, the hotel's own Savoy Blend is the most popular choice, along with Earl Grey. It also offers a collection of fine teas from the reputed tea merchant Newby Teas:

Assam (India), with 'a mild, slightly nutty aroma which belies its assertive taste. The strength and maltiness of Assam makes a perfect tea to wake up your senses at breakfast.'

Darjeeling (Himalayas). A broken Orange Pekoe tea with a pale amber liquor and floral fruity nose. Its delicate flavour has a hint of Moscatel grapes.

Earl Grey (China and Darjeeling). An unusual blend of China and Darjeeling teas, with a quite wonderful aroma. Introduced to England in the 1830s.

Lapsang Souchong (China). A large leaf tea with a pungent smoky or tarry flavour, produced by withering Souchong leaves over open pine fires.

Plus speciality blends from the famous tea rooms of Mariage Freres in Paris:

Marco Polo. A blend from China and Tibet, perfumed with fruits and flowers.

Casablanca. A blend of Moroccan green tea perfumed with mint and bergamot.

Herbal teas: Mint, Camomile, Lime Flower.

And, in case you are wondering, the Savoy Blend is made up of Pure Assam and Broken Orange Pekoe tea. The special blend was originally selected and voted in by the Savoy directors. Over the years, the quality of the Assam may have changed, but the proportions used in the blend are adhered to by the hotel's modern-day suppliers.

Anton Edelmann says, 'Afternoon tea is terribly civilised. I always think that if you go to have afternoon tea, you've made it. I walk through in the afternoon and think "What a marvellous thing to do, to take two hours out and sit there, listen to a little bit of piano, eat a little sandwich and the odd pastry". I always imagine it would be very nice.'

pear custard tarts

Makes 6

150 ml/5 fl oz/⅔ cup double cream (heavy cream)

2 vanilla pods (vanilla beans), split

2 eggs

1 egg yolk

360 g/12 oz/1¾ cups caster sugar (US granulated sugar)

2 pears, peeled

4 tbsp Poire William's liqueur

300 g/10½ oz Sweet Pastry (see page 92)

3 tbsp apricot jam

Put the cream and 1 vanilla pod in a pan and bring just to the boil. In a bowl, beat together the eggs, egg yolk and 60 g/2 oz/5 tbsp of the sugar until fluffy. Add the hot cream, stirring contantly. Strain, then leave to cool.

Put the remaining sugar and vanilla pod in another saucepan and add 500 ml/16 fl oz/2 cups water. Bring to the boil, stirring to dissolve the sugar. Add the pears. Cover with greaseproof paper (wax paper) to keep the fruit immersed. Simmer gently for about 25 minutes or until the pears are soft but not mushy – check with a small knife. Add the Poire William's, then leave the pears to cool in the syrup.

Roll out the pastry to 3 mm/⅛ inch thick, and line six 7.5 cm/3 inch tartlet moulds. Allow to rest in the refrigerator for 20 minutes.

Heat the oven to 180°C/350°F/gas mark 4.

Line the pastry cases with greaseproof paper or baking parchment and fill with baking beans. Bake blind for 10 minutes. Remove the paper and baking beans, then bake for a further 4 minutes. Cool. Reduce the heat of the oven to 150°C/300°F/gas mark 2.

Drain the pears (keep the poaching syrup for a fruit salad) and cut them in half lengthways. Remove the stalk and core, and cut across into 3 mm/⅛ inch thick slices. Arrange in the tartlet cases. Fill to the top with the vanilla custard and bake for 20 minutes. Cool before removing from the moulds.

Heat the apricot jam until melted, and brush on to the tarts to glaze.

'Nowhere is the English genius for domesticity more notably evidenced than in the festival of afternoon tea.'

George Gissing

raspberry mille-feuilles

Makes 4

250 g/8½ oz Puff Pastry
(see page 91)

100 g/3½ oz/1 cup icing sugar
(confectioners' sugar)

200 ml/7 fl oz/1 cup double cream
(heavy cream), whipped

24 raspberries

On a lightly floured surface, roll out the pastry very thinly (no more than 3 mm/⅛ inch thick). Cut out three rectangles, each 9 x 20 cm/3½ x 8 inches. Place them on lightly greased baking trays and prick well with a fork. Rest for 20 minutes in a cool place.

Heat the oven to 200°C/400°F/gas mark 6.

Bake the pastry strips for about 5 minutes or until golden brown and crisp. Allow to cool.

Preheat the grill (broiler).

Dust the pastry evenly with half of the icing sugar and caramelise under the grill.

Spread one of the pastry strips with the cream and arrange 12 of the raspberries over the surface. Place a second strip on this and spread on the remainder of the cream and raspberries. Top this with the final strip of pastry, sugared side down. Press down lightly and trim uneven edges from the sides.

Refrigerate for 20 minutes, then slice across evenly into 4. Dust with the remaining icing sugar.

royal biscuits

Makes 8

400 g/14 oz Puff Pastry
(see page 91)

1 egg white

500 g/1 lb 2 oz/4 cups icing sugar
(confectioners' sugar)

On a lightly floured surface roll out the pastry into a 5 x 30 cm/2 x 12 inch rectangle that is 3 mm/⅛ inch thick. Transfer to a tray. Prick well with a fork and rest in the refrigerator for 20 minutes.

Beat the egg white and icing sugar together with a wooden spoon until smooth. Spread thinly on to the chilled pastry. Freeze for 25 minutes.

Heat the oven to 220°C/425°F/gas mark 7.

Cut into 8 fingers, using a damp knife each time, and place on a baking tray lined with greaseproof paper or baking parchment. Bake for about 15 minutes. The icing should curl up at the ends and the pastry should be golden.

savoy choux pastry swans

Makes 10

150 g/5 oz Choux Pastry
(see page 90)

25 g/l oz/2 tbsp caster sugar
(US granulated sugar)

750 ml/1¼ pints/3 cups double
cream (heavy cream)

icing sugar (confectioners' sugar)
to dust

Heat the oven to 200°C/400°F/gas
mark 6.

Using a 1 cm/½ inch nozzle, pipe ten
2.5 cm/1 inch diameter rounds of
choux pastry on to a buttered baking
tray. Bake the buns for 15 minutes.
Cool.

Using a 3 mm/⅛ inch nozzle, pipe
ten 'S' shapes of choux pastry on
another buttered baking tray. Reduce
the oven heat to 180°C/350°F/gas
mark 4, and bake for 10 minutes or
until golden brown and crispy. Cool.

Split the buns in half horizontally,
then cut the tops in half.

Add the sugar to the cream and
whip until just firm. Use a small star
nozzle to fill the base of the choux
buns with whipped cream. Place the
top halves in the cream at an angle,
to give the impression of wings.
Place the 'S' shaped pieces of choux
at the front of each bun, for the
swan's neck. Dust each swan with
icing sugar.

strawberry tartlets

Makes 6

3 sheets filo pastry, each about
30 x 35 cm/10 x 14 inches

20 g/scant ¼ oz/1½ tbsp unsalted
butter, melted

½ quantity Frangipane
see page 90)

2 tsp crème de framboise liqueur
(optional)

4 tbsp Pastry Cream (see page 88)
or whipped cream

14 medium strawberries, hulled

4 tbsp strawberry jam

a few skinned and chopped pistachio
nuts to decorate

Heat the oven to 200°C/400°F/gas
mark 6.

Brush one sheet of filo pastry with
some of the melted butter. Lay
another sheet of filo on top and
brush with more butter, then add
the final sheet and brush with the

last of the butter. Cut out six 9–10
cm/3½–4 inch rounds and use to line
six 7.5 cm/3 inch tartlet tins. Divide
the frangipane among the pastry
cases. Bake for about 10 minutes or
until golden. Leave to cool.

Stir the framboise liqueur, if using,
into the pastry cream or whipped
cream. Spoon on to the centre of
each tartlet, keeping it away from
the edges or it will flow out when
the fruit is pressed on. Place a whole
strawberry in the centre of each tart.
Cut the rest of the strawberries in
half and arrange around the whole
ones.

Warm the strawberry jam until
melted, then, if necessary, press it
through a fine sieve to remove bits
of fruit. Brush the strawberries with
the jam to glaze them, then sprinkle
a few chopped pistachios on top.

traditional french orange tart

Makes a
20 cm/8 inch tart

170 g/6 oz Sweet Pastry
(see page 92)

4 egg yolks

15 g/½ oz/2 tbsp cornflour
(cornstarch)

160 ml/5½ fl oz/¾ cup orange juice

grated zest of 1 orange

120 g/4 oz/½ cup + 2 tbsp sugar

50 g/1¾ oz/3½ tbsp soft unsalted
butter

icing sugar (confectioners' sugar)
to dust

Roll out the pastry on a lightly
floured surface and use to line a
20 cm/8 inch loose-based flan tin.
Line the pastry case with
greaseproof paper or baking
parchment and fill with baking
beans. Chill for 20 minutes.

Heat the oven to 200°C/400°F/gas
mark 6.

Bake the pastry case for 10 minutes,
then remove the paper and beans.
Brush the pastry lightly with a little

egg yolk and bake for a further
10 minutes or until golden brown.
Set aside.

Mix the cornflour with a little of the
orange juice. Put the remaining juice
in a pan with the zest and 100 g/
3½ oz/½ cup of the sugar and bring
to the boil. Add the cornflour and
bring back to the boil, stirring.

Whisk the remaining egg yolks with
the remaining sugar until smooth.
Add to the orange mixture and whisk
vigorously until smooth, then bring
to the boil again. Remove from the
heat and whisk in the butter. Pour
into the flan case.

Lower the heat of the oven to
150°C/300°F/gas mark 2 and bake
the tart for 40 minutes.

Dust heavily with icing sugar and
caramelise with a blowtorch or
under a very hot grill (broiler),
taking care not to burn the edge of
the pastry case.

walnut pie

*Makes a
20 cm/8 inch pie*

250g/8½ oz Sweet Pastry
(see page 92)

300 g/10 oz/2 cups walnut halves

3 eggs

150 g/5 oz/¾ cup soft brown sugar

75 g/2½ oz/5 tbsp unsalted butter,
melted

100 g/3½ oz/⅓ cup golden syrup or
dark corn syrup

Preheat the oven to 170°C/325°F/gas
mark 3.

On a lightly floured surface, roll out
the pastry and use to line a deep
20 cm/8 inch loose-based flan tin.
Set aside.

Reserve 50 g/1¾ oz/⅓ cup of the
walnut halves, and put the rest in a
food processor with the eggs, sugar,
melted butter and syrup. Blend until
the walnuts are coarsely chopped.
Pour into the pastry case. Arrange
the reserved walnut halves on top.

Bake for about 1 hour or until the
filling is set and the pastry is golden
brown. Serve warm or cool.

brûlee cappuccino

Serves 8

350 ml/12 fl oz/1½ cups double cream

70 ml/2½ fl oz/5 tbsp milk

3 egg yolks

80 g/2¾ oz/6½ tbsp sugar

2 tsp instant coffee, dissolved in a few drops of water

60 g/2 oz milk chocolate

100 g/3½ oz/½ cup dark brown sugar

Heat the oven to 150°C/300°F/gas mark 2.

In a saucepan bring the cream and milk to the boil. Lightly mix the egg yolks and sugar together, then pour in the cream mixture and the coffee, stirring constantly. Add the chocolate and stir until it has melted. Pass through a fine sieve.

Pour the custard into 8 small dishes or ramekins that are about 7 cm/ 3 inches wide and 2 cm/¾ inch deep. Set them in a bain marie or roasting tin of water and bake for 30 minutes.

Remove from the bain marie and allow to cool for 10 minutes.

Preheat the grill (broiler).

Sprinkle the top of each custard with an even layer of dark brown sugar. Place under the hot grill until the sugar melts and caramelises. Leave to cool and set before serving.

pineapple and ginger cakes

Makes 8

1 large pineapple

100 g/3½ oz/½ cup caster sugar (US granulated sugar)

120 g/4 oz/8 tbsp unsalted butter

2 tbsp chopped preserved stem ginger

120 g/4 oz/¾ cup + 2 tbsp plain flour (all-purpose flour)

½ tsp bicarbonate of soda (baking soda)

½ tsp baking powder

pinch of salt

150 g/5 oz/¾ cup soft brown sugar

2 eggs

1 tsp pure vanilla extract

100 ml/3½ fl oz/7 tbsp crème fraîche

Heat the oven to 190°C/375°F/gas mark 5. Butter 8 deep 10 cm/4 inch ramekin dishes. If you wish, line the bottoms with baking parchment.

Peel the pineapple and cut 8 slices about 1.5 cm/⅝ inch thick. Remove the core from the centre of each slice. Trim them so they will fit exactly in the bottom of the ramekins. Reserve all the trimmings of pineapple and finely chop them – you should have 150–200 g/5–7 oz/about 1 cup finely chopped bits.

Put the caster sugar in a heavy-based saucepan with one-third of the butter. Heat until melted, then cook until it is a medium deep brown colour. Divide this caramel between the ramekin dishes and sprinkle with the chopped ginger. Set a slice of pineapple in each one.

Sift the flour, bicarbonate of soda, baking powder and salt together. Beat together the brown sugar and the remaining butter until creamy. Beat in the eggs one at a time, then add the vanilla extract. Fold in the flour mixture until well combined, then stir in the crème fraîche and the reserved finely chopped pineapple.

Divide the mixture among the ramekins and level the surface. Bake for about 25 minutes or until firm.

Leave until the dishes are cool enough to handle, then unmould carefully, pineapple side up. Serve warm.

c o f f e e   t o o ...

You can, of course, drink coffee with your cake and sandwiches. Anton Edelmann remembers how the hotel used to procure its beans. 'When I came here, we roasted our own coffee in Covent Garden. It was done by a Polish man who was 78 and could hardly see. We had four varieties in sacks and he had a tin, like an old peas tin, and in there he had last week's coffee. He'd take out a handful of beans, look at them, then try to mix them to the same colour. That's how we got the Royal warrant for our coffee!'

hot chocolate pudding

Serves 4

150 g/5 oz plain chocolate (semisweet chocolate)

15 g/½ oz/1 tbsp unsalted butter

3 eggs, separated

3 tbsp caster sugar (US granulated sugar)

icing sugar (confectioners' sugar) to finish

Melt the chocolate with the butter in a heavy-based saucepan over very low heat. Pour into a bowl. Beat the egg yolks into the melted chocolate.

In a large clean bowl, whisk the egg whites with the sugar to a stiff peak. Stir a spoonful of the whites into the chocolate mixture to loosen it, then fold in the remaining whites with a metal spoon. Cover and refrigerate for 1½–2 hours.

Heat the oven to 220°C/425°F/gas mark 7. Generously butter the inside of four 8.5 cm/3½ inch diameter ramekins.

Spoon the chocolate mixture into the ramekins (it should come to 5 mm/¼ inch from the top). Bake for 15 minutes or until risen. Remove from the oven and set aside in a warm place to rest for 15 minutes.

Loosen the sides of each pudding with a small sharp knife, then turn it out into your hand. Set the pudding right side up in the centre of a warmed plate. Dust lightly with icing sugar and serve.

the light fantastic

Memories of tea and cakes can be so evocative. As Marcel Proust said in *Remembrance of Things Past*, 'And suddenly the memory revealed itself. The taste was that of the little crumb of madeleine which on Sunday mornings at Combray…when I used to say goodbye to her in her bedroom, my aunt Leonie used to give me, dipping it first in her own cup of real or of limewater tea.' Rupert Brooke reminisced fondly while fighting in the First World war: 'Stands the Church clock at ten to three? And is there honey still for tea? – using afternoon tea as a metaphor for England and familiar, well-loved traditions.

Tea as a meal was introduced to this country by Anna, 7th Duchess of Bedford, in the early 1800s, as a means of filling the gap between an early luncheon and a late dinner. Head Chef Anton Edelmann believes that it shouldn't be too filling. 'For example, we do small crème brûlées – pistachio and so on. You have just two or three teaspoonfuls and it's gone.

'I have been at The Savoy for 17 years and in that time we have made afternoon tea smaller, more delicate-looking. All the cakes, scones and pastries are made in our patisserie here

'Thank God for tea! What would the world do without tea? How did it exist? I am glad I was not born before tea.'

The Reverend Sidney Smith

at the hotel. The pastry is now thinner and we've introduced different fruit into the tarts: summer fruit, exotic fruit in winter, apples and pears in autumn. We also have a lighter fruit cake in the summer, but in winter revert to the heavier variety and offer Madeira and Dundee cake as well. Two years ago we did a buffet with seven or eight summer fruit tarts with things like loganberries and blueberries and guests could go up and help themselves instead of sitting down all the time.

plus ça change

Woe betide anyone who tries to interfere with the ritual of afternoon tea – after all, we have all come to expect a panoply of sandwiches, cakes, scones and pots of tea. But The Savoy has stayed one step ahead of the rest by ringing the changes on a regular basis. For example, instead of a simple choice between brown and white bread (crusts removed), a baker makes up daily batches of sage and tomato bread to Anton Edelmann's own recipe. Scones, too, are given a delicious twist. As well as apple and cinnamon, guests have enjoyed raisin and even walnut varieties.

a p r i c o t   a n d   p e c a n   s t i c k y   b u n s

Makes 10

100 ml/3½ fl oz/7 tbsp milk, heated until tepid

10 g/⅓ oz/1 cake fresh yeast

125 g/4¼ oz/½ cup + 2 tbsp sugar

170 g/6 oz/1½ cups strong white flour (bread flour), sifted

55 g/2 oz/4 tbsp butter

pinch of salt

2 eggs

70 g/2¼ oz/½ cup dried apricots, chopped

6 pecan nuts, chopped

100 ml/3½ fl oz/7 tbsp water

Mix together the milk, yeast, 25 g/¾ oz/2 tbsp of the sugar and one-third of the flour. Cover and leave in a warm place to rise.

Rub the remaining flour with the butter and salt until a fine crumble is formed. Make a well in the centre and add the eggs, apricots, pecan nuts and milk dough. Knead together until evenly combined. Cover and leave in a warm place until doubled in volume.

Knock back (punch down) the dough. Cover again and leave to rise until doubled in volume once more.

Cut the dough into 25 g/¾ oz pieces and mould into buns or into finger shapes. Place on a greased baking sheet and leave in a warm place for 25 minutes or until doubled in volume.

Heat the oven to 230°C/450°F/gas mark 8.

Bake the buns for 10 minutes.

Heat the remaining sugar with the water, stirring until dissolved, and bring to the boil. Remove the buns from the oven and brush with the sugar syrup.

d o u g h n u t s

Makes 6

200 ml/7 fl oz/⅞ cup milk

12 g/½ oz/1 cake fresh yeast

50 g/1¾ oz/1/4 cup caster sugar
(US granulated sugar)

360 g/12½ oz/3 cups strong white
flour (bread flour)

pinch of salt

70 g/2¼ oz/5 tbsp butter

1 egg

oil for deep-frying

50 g/1¾ oz/3 tbsp jam

caster sugar (US granulated sugar)
to finish

Warm the milk to blood temperature.
Add the yeast and sugar, and stir to
dissolve. Sprinkle on 120 g/4 oz/
1 cup of the flour. Leave in a warm
place for 1 hour.

Sift the remaining flour and salt into
a bowl. Rub in the butter, then form
a well in the centre. Add the yeast
mixture and the egg. Knead well to a
firm and smooth dough. Cover with

a damp cloth and leave in a warm
place for 20 minutes or until the
volume has increased by one-third.

Remove the dough from the bowl
and knock back (punch down).
Return to the bowl, cover and leave
in a warm place to increase in
volume again.

Cut the dough into 50 g/1¾ oz
pieces and roll into balls. Place on a
floured tray. Leave in a warm place
until the volume has doubled.

Heat oil for deep-frying to
175°C/345°F. Gently remove the
doughnuts with a palette knife
(metal spatula) and immerse in the
hot oil. They should immediately rise
to the surface. Turn the doughnuts
over after a few minutes. Total frying
time is 8–10 minutes. When cooked,
remove from the oil with a draining
spoon and place on kitchen paper
towels to drain.

Puncture each doughnut and pipe in
the jam, then roll in caster sugar.

m u f f i n s

Makes 12

8 tbsp mild vegetable oil

8 tbsp water

2 tsp honey

2 eggs

2 tsp liquid glucose

150 g/5 oz/1 cup plain flour
(all-purpose flour)

1 tbsp cornflour (cornstarch)

120 g/4¼ oz/½ cup + 2 tbsp caster
sugar (US granulated sugar)

2 tsp baking powder

pinch of salt

Heat the oven to 200°C/400°F/gas
mark 6.

Mix together the oil, water, honey,
eggs and glucose in the bowl of an
electric mixer. Add all the other
ingredients and beat on high speed
for 8 minutes. Gently fold in the
flavouring of your choice (see right).

Spoon the mixture into doubled
paper baking cases set in muffin
tins, filling just above half way.
Place in the oven and bake for
18 minutes.

When cooked take the muffins out of
the tins, leaving the outside paper
case behind.

Optional flavourings
40 g/1½ oz/¼ cup blueberries
or
20 g/⅔ oz/3 tbsp grated carrots and
20 g/⅔ oz/3 tbsp chopped walnuts
or
30 g/1 oz/3 tbsp chocolate chips and
2 tbsp unsweetened cocoa powder

a   t o p - d r a w e r   d r i n k

Tea has always been seen as the drink for the aristocracy, largely because it used to be a luxury item, kept locked in caddies to prevent theft. As GK Chesterton so succinctly put it: 'Tea, although an Oriental/Is a gentleman at least;/Cocoa is a cad and a coward,/Cocoa is a vulgar beast.

And Charles Oliver, in Dinner at Buckingham Palace, writes: 'The ritual of the English teatime was brought to perfection by the late Queen Mary… Everything had to be fully ready by 4pm punctually, with sandwiches, cakes and biscuits invitingly set out on gleaming silver dishes upon a smoothly-running trolley. The teapot, cream jug, hot-water jug and sugar bowl were always the same antique silver service which had been a favourite of Queen Victoria… Queen Mary would take over and meticulously measure out her favourite Indian tea from a jade tea-caddy she kept locked in a cupboard. Then she would pour on the boiling water and complete the tea-making ritual by snuffing out the spirit stove before sitting back for the footmen to pour tea and hand round sandwiches and cakes. But before Queen Mary gave the signal for this to begin she would always let exactly three minutes elapse from the moment she poured hot water on to the leaves so that the tea would be perfectly brewed.'

scones

Makes 8

220 g/7¾ oz/1½ cups plain flour (all-purpose flour)

15 g/½ oz/4 tsp baking powder

75 g/2½ oz/5 tbsp butter

60 g/2 oz/5 tbsp caster sugar (US granulated sugar)

150 ml/5 fl oz/⅔ cup milk

1 egg yolk, lightly beaten, to glaze

Heat the oven to 200°C/400°F/ gas mark 6.

Sift the flour and baking powder into a bowl. Rub the butter and sugar into the flour to form a fine crumble. Make a well in the centre and add the milk (and optional flavourings such as sultanas, cherries, pecan nuts or apple). Knead gently together, being careful not to overmix.

On a lightly floured surface roll out the dough to 1.5 cm/⅝ inch thickness. Stamp out 6 cm/2½ inch rounds with a plain pastry cutter.

Place on a greased baking sheet and brush the tops with the egg yolk. Allow to stand for 15 minutes.

Bake for 12–15 minutes or until risen and lightly golden on top.

Serve warm, with clotted cream and strawberry jam.

Optional flavourings
80 g/2¾ oz/⅔ cup pecan nuts, chopped
or
60 g/2 oz/½ cup sultanas (golden raisins)
or
50 g/1¾ oz/⅓ cup glacé cherries (candied cherries), chopped
or
80 g/2¾ oz/⅔ cup peeled and diced apple

cottage cheese and pineapple
sandwiches

Makes 6 finger sandwiches

150 g/5 oz/⅔ cup cottage cheese

100 g/3½ oz/1 cup pineapple, finely diced

4 slices of brown bread, buttered

freshly ground pepper

Mix together the cottage cheese and pineapple, then season with pepper. Make into 2 sandwiches with the bread. Cut off the crusts and cut each sandwich into 3 equal fingers.

cream cheese and marmite
sandwiches

Makes 8 small square sandwiches

4 slices of white bread

2–3 tsp Marmite

80 g/2¾ oz/⅓ cup cream cheese, such as Philadelphia

Toast the bread. Spread two slices very thinly with the Marmite. Spread the cream cheese on the other two slices and put together with the Marmite slices to make sandwiches. Cut off the crusts and cut each sandwich into squares.

cheese puffs with guacamole

Makes 12

200 g/7 oz Puff Pastry (see page 91)

30 g/1 oz/¼ cup Parmesan cheese, freshly grated

½ tsp paprika

1 egg, lightly beaten

small amount of sesame seeds

small amount of poppy seeds

For the guacamole

1 ripe avocado

¼ clove garlic, crushed

½ large onion, peeled and finely chopped

½ spring onion (green onion), finely chopped

1 tomato, seeded, drained and finely chopped

juice of ½ lemon

1 tsp Tabasco sauce

pinch of cayenne pepper or hot chilli powder

pinch of ground cumin

pinch of celery salt

pinch of white pepper

Roll out the puff pastry to about 1 cm/½ inch thick. Sprinkle evenly with the Parmesan, then continue rolling out to 3 mm/⅛ inch thickness. With a 6 cm/2½ inch diameter cutter, stamp out 12 rounds. Sprinkle them lightly with the paprika. Brush the tops with beaten egg wash and leave to rest in the refrigerator for 20 minutes.

Heat the oven to 200°C/400°F/gas mark 6.

Brush once more with beaten egg. Sprinkle half of the rounds with sesame seeds and the other half with poppy seeds. Bake for about 15 minutes. Leave to cool, then cut the puffs in half horizontally.

For the guacamole, halve the
avocado, discard the stone and
scoop out the flesh into a bowl.
Mash lightly. Add the garlic, onions,
tomato, lemon juice, Tabasco and

spices, and mix thoroughly. Check
the seasoning and adjust if necessary.

Fill the puffs with the guacamole and
top with the seeded tops.

a select choice of morsels

The three-tiered silver cake stand bears a select choice of morsels. Which sandwich to start? Choose from prawn and mayonnaise; egg, cucumber and mint; tomato, cream cheese and basil; ham, mustard and mayonnaise or smoked salmon, all light and generously plump, some presented on The Savoy's own tomato and sage breads. Then follows fresh baked scones, in a variety of flavours, made at the hotel. You add your own jam – high-quality strawberry (what else?) – and a dollop of rich, yellow clotted cream. The finale consists of jewel-like patisserie, also made at the hotel – tiny confections of chocolate, sponge and crème patissière, presented like works of art in crinkled paper cases that rustle pleasingly as you cut into them.

creamed avocado sandwiches with plum tomato and red onion

Makes 6 finger sandwiches

1 avocado, peeled and stoned

4 tbsp crème fraîche

2 plum tomatoes, peeled, seeded and finely diced

1 small red onion, peeled and finely chopped

salt and freshly ground pepper

4 slices of brown bread, buttered

Mash the avocado with the crème fraîche. Stir in the diced tomato and red onion, and season to taste. Fill the bread with this mixture to make 2 sandwiches. Cut off the crusts and cut each sandwich into 3 equal fingers.

cucumber sandwiches with egg and mint

Makes 6 finger sandwiches

2 hard-boiled eggs, peeled and finely grated

2 tbsp crème fraîche

½ bunch of fresh mint, leaves picked and finely chopped

salt and freshly ground pepper

4 slices of white bread, buttered

½ cucumber (English cucumber), peeled and finely sliced

Mix the eggs with the crème fraîche and mint. Season with salt and pepper. Spread 5 mm/¼ inch thick on 2 slices of bread. Top with the sliced cucumber and cover with the remaining slices of bread.

Remove the crusts and cut each sandwich into 3 equal fingers.

herb scones with white crab meat and keta caviar

Makes 6

250 g/8½ oz/2 cups strong white flour (bread flour)

15 g/½ oz/4 tsp baking powder

75 g/2½ oz/5 tbsp unsalted butter

4 tsp chopped mixed fresh herbs, such as basil, rosemary, marjoram and oregano

120 ml/4 fl oz/½ cup milk

1 egg, lightly beaten

For the filling

100 ml/3½ fl oz/7 tbsp crème fraîche

150 g/5 oz/1½ cups white crab meat

60 g/2 oz/⅓ cup cucumber, seeded and diced

salt and freshly ground pepper

mixed lettuce and fresh dill to garnish

1 tbsp keta caviar

Heat the oven to 200°C/400°F/gas mark 6.

Sift the flour and baking powder into a bowl, then rub in the butter until the mixture resembles breadcrumbs. Stir in the herbs. Add the milk and work to a soft dough.

On a lightly floured surface, roll out the dough to 2 cm/¾ inch thick. Stamp out 6 cm/2½ inch rounds with a cutter. Transfer to a greased baking sheet and brush the tops with beaten egg. Bake for about 15 minutes or until risen and golden brown. Allow to cool.

Mix the crème fraîche with the crab meat and cucumber. Season with salt and pepper. Arrange a few small lettuce leaves on the edge of each scone. Heap a generous amount of crab meat on each, add a small spoonful of caviar and garnish the top with sprigs of dill.

honey and ham biscuits

Makes about 16

20 g/¾ oz/1½ tbsp finely chopped onion

½ tsp olive oil

2 cloves garlic, peeled and crushed

45 g/1½ oz/3 tbsp unsalted butter, at room temperature

1 tsp English mustard

1 egg yolk

4 tsp Acacia honey

50 g/1¾ oz/⅓ cup cooked ham, finely chopped

45 g/1½ oz/⅓ cup Cheddar cheese, grated

90 g/3 oz/½ cup + 2 tbsp plain flour (all-purpose flour)

Sweat the onion in the oil until soft and translucent. Add the garlic and sweat for a further minute, then leave to cool.

Beat the butter until creamy and then stir in the mustard and egg yolk. Add the onion and garlic, the honey, ham, cheese and flour, and mix until evenly combined to a dough. Wrap in cling film (plastic wrap) and chill for 20 minutes.

Heat the oven to 190°C/375°F/gas mark 5.

Roll out the dough on a lightly floured surface to 5–6 mm/¼ inch thick. Stamp out 6 cm/2½ inch rounds. Place on a greased baking tray and bake for about 20 minutes or until golden. Cool on a wire rack.

prawn and spring onion sandwiches with sun-dried tomato bread

Makes 6 finger sandwiches

100 g/3½ oz/1 cup peeled, cooked prawns (small shrimp)

2 spring onions (green onions), finely chopped

2 tbsp mayonnaise-based cocktail sauce

salt and freshly ground pepper

4 slices of sun-dried tomato bread, buttered

Mix together the prawns, spring onions and cocktail sauce, and season with salt and pepper. Make into 2 sandwiches with the bread. Cut off the crusts and cut each sandwich into 3 equal fingers.

roast beef sandwiches with horseradish cream

Makes 6 finger sandwiches

2 tbsp crème fraîche

1 tsp finely grated fresh horseradish

4 slices of brown bread, buttered

4 slices of roast beef

salt and freshly ground pepper

Mix the crème fraîche and horseradish together and spread evenly over the slices of bread. Arrange the roast beef on top of half of the slices and season to taste. Put the other slices of bread on the beef. Cut off the crusts and cut each sandwich into 3 equal fingers.

how do we like it?

For many centuries, China supplied most of the world's tea and, indeed, was the birthplace of tea. According to Chinese mythology, in 2737BC Emperor Shen Nung was sitting beneath a tree while his manservant boiled drinking water. A leaf from a wild tea tree fell in, and Nung, a herbalist, decided to try it. As tea grew in popularity, it was cultivated throughout China and Japan, but only arrived in Europe in the 17th century, as sea routes opened up with the Far East.

Today, however, most of the tea drunk in Britain is black tea, from Kenya, which supplies more tea to Britain than both India and Sri Lanka (Ceylon). Although China supplies semi-fermented oolong teas which are halfway between black and green tea, the market for its green tea (Lapsang Souchong, Yunnan, Keemun and Gunpowder) is much smaller and more specialised.

Interestingly, despite the growth of coffee bars in recent years, tea is still the drink of choice in this country. Every day, 37 million of us drink tea, choosing maltier, richer brews at breakfast time and lighter, more fragrant tea in the afternoon – one reason why The Savoy special blend contains fragrant Orange Pekoe as well as more substantial Assam.

Tea is also being touted as a great protector of health. Containing vitamins, minerals and antioxidants, some research claims that it helps to protect against certain cancers, strokes and heart disease. What better reason for enjoying afternoon tea?

tea and tangos

The Savoy has recently resurrected the idea of the tea dance, popular in the early 1900s, when ladies were required to wear 'afternoon street dress with hats'. And, in a nod to this earlier era, a complimentary glass of champagne is given to anyone who goes tea dancing wearing a hat! Legendary bandleader Victor Sylvester led the Savoy Orpheans and Rudolph Valentino's first public appearances at The Savoy were when he danced at the thé dansant afternoons; in addition, a member of the Strauss family was the first artist hired by The Savoy to provide music while guests dined, the idea being 'to cover the silence which hangs over an English dining table.' Modern-day guests dance to a four-piece band playing popular waltzes and tangoes, and enjoy a full afternoon tea.

smoked salmon bagels

Makes 8

2 bagels, sliced horizontally in half and each half cut across in half

4 tbsp crème fraîche

2 tsp freshly grated horseradish or 4 tsp creamed horseradish

4 large slices of smoked salmon, cut in half

freshly ground black pepper

4 slices of smoked bacon (optional)

1 punnet mustard and cress (garden cress)

Toast the bagel pieces under the grill (broiler) on the cut side. Mix the crème fraîche with the horseradish and spread over the bagels. Top with the smoked salmon. Grind a small amount of pepper on each.

If using the bacon, grill (broil) it and cut each slice in half. Arrange a piece on top of each bagel and sprinkle with the mustard and cress.

Sandwiches are, of course, a staple of the afternoon tea menu and should be as fresh as possible. Anton Edelmann says, 'There are things that have to be in the sandwiches – fillings like eggs, tomato. We have done prawn with guacamole, though. Bread should be very fresh and buttered sparingly, so that sandwiches are feather light.' Fortunately, he hasn't gone down the line chosen by the Beatles, who ordered pea sandwiches when staying at The Savoy…

cheese sablés

Makes about 20

150 g/5 oz/1 cup plain flour
(all-purpose flour)

150 g/5 oz/1½ cups Parmesan
cheese, freshly grated

150 g/5 oz/10 tbsp butter

1 egg yolk

Mix the flour and cheese together in a bowl, then work in the butter with your fingertips until evenly mixed. Work in the egg yolk to form a firm dough. Wrap the dough and leave to rest in a cool place for about 30 minutes.

Heat the oven to 200°C/400°F/gas mark 6.

On a lightly floured surface, roll out the dough until it is 5–6 mm/¼ inch thick. Stamp out 6 cm/2½ inch rounds and place on baking sheets. Bake for about 20 minutes or until golden, then cool on a wire rack.

spinach and cheddar eccles

Makes 4

20 g/¼ oz/1½ tbsp unsalted butter

30 g/l oz/¼ cup peeled and finely chopped apple

1 tsp lemon juice

½ onion, peeled and finely chopped

2 tbsp vegetable oil

50 g/1¾ oz/¼ cup spinach, blanched, squeezed dry and roughly chopped

salt and freshly ground pepper

90 g/3 oz/⅔ cup Cheddar cheese, coarsely crumbled

45 g/1½ oz/¼ cup raisins

200 g/7 oz Puff Pastry (see page 91)

1 egg, beaten

Melt the butter in a small pan, add the apple and lemon juice, and sweat until softened.

In a separate pan, sweat the onion in the oil until soft and translucent. Add the spinach and season with salt and pepper. Leave to cool, then stir in the Cheddar, softened apple mixture and raisins.

On a lightly floured surface, roll out the puff pastry to about 3 mm/ ⅛ inch thick. Stamp out four 15 cm/ 6 inch rounds. Divide the filling among the pastry rounds, piling it in the centre. Brush the pastry edges with water, then bring them up over the filling to encase it completely. Press the edges together in the centre to seal firmly.

Turn the pastries over so that the sealed edges are underneath, then roll them out gently until they are about 2.5 cm/1 inch thick. Brush the tops with beaten egg and make 2 small cuts in each one. Place the pastries on a greased baking tray and leave to rest in a cool place for 15 minutes.

Heat the oven to 200°C/400°F/gas mark 6.

Bake the pastries for about 20 minutes or until golden brown. Serve warm.

Anton Edelmann: 'I think people should ring the changes as they do with wine. But, instead they drink the same old brew all the time. I've often thought of having a tea trolley here with four or five different varieties – you could have Earl Grey, then something else.

tomato snails

Makes 24

225 g/8 oz/1⅔ cups plain flour
(all-purpose flour)

50 g/1¼ oz/3½ tbsp unsalted butter

45 g/1½ oz/3 tbsp cream cheese

1 egg yolk

For the filling

100 g/3½ oz/1 cup pecorino cheese,
grated

90 g/3 oz/heaped ⅓ cup sun-dried
tomatoes in olive oil, drained

100 g/3½ oz (2 cans) anchovy fillets,
drained and chopped

90 g/3 oz/⅔ cup pitted black olives,
chopped

The dough can be prepared a day in
advance. Alternatively you can make
the snails and freeze them, then
thaw and bake whenever required.

Sift the flour into a bowl and rub in
the butter and cream cheese until
the mixture resembles fine crumbs.
Add the egg yolk and sufficient cold
water to form a soft, smooth dough.
Wrap and refrigerate for 20 minutes.

Heat the oven to 200°C/400°F/gas
mark 6.

On a lightly floured surface, roll out
the dough to a 35 x 30 cm/14 x 12
inch rectangle. Sprinkle it evenly
with the cheese, then arrange the
remaining ingredients on top. Roll
up the dough like a Swiss roll (jelly
roll), starting at a long side, and cut
it into slices 1.5 cm/⅝ inch thick.
Arrange on a greased baking tray,
cut side up, and bake for about
20 minutes or until golden brown.
Serve warm.

swiss mushroom rarebit

Serves 4

8 medium open-cap mushrooms

2 shallots, peeled and finely chopped

120 g/4 oz/8 tbsp unsalted butter

250 g/8½ oz/3 cups button mushrooms, finely chopped

salt and freshly ground pepper

100 ml/3½ fl oz/7 tbsp dry white wine

2 tbsp plain flour (all-purpose flour)

200 ml/7 fl oz/⅞ cup milk

50 g/1¼ oz/½ cup Emmenthal cheese, grated

2 egg yolks

1 tsp Dijon mustard

1 tbsp double cream (heavy cream)

cayenne pepper

Worcestershire sauce

4 slices of white bread

Wipe the open-cap mushrooms. Remove the stalks and chop them finely, reserving the mushroom caps.

Sweat the shallots in 45 g/1½ oz/ 3 tbsp of the butter until soft and translucent. Add the button mushrooms and chopped mushroom stalks and sweat for a further minute. Season with salt and pepper, then add 1 teaspoon of the white wine and cook slowly until all the liquid has evaporated.

Melt the remaining butter in a small, heavy-based pan and add the flour. Stir over a medium heat for 2 minutes, then pour in the remaining wine and the milk, stirring constantly. The mixture may curdle at this stage because of the wine, but don't worry – keep cooking it! Simmer for 2–3 minutes, stirring frequently, to give a smooth sauce. If there are any lumps, you can pass the sauce though a fine sieve.

Remove from the heat and add three-quarters of the grated cheese, plus the egg yolks, mustard and cream. Add cayenne pepper and Worcestershire sauce to taste.

Preheat the grill (broiler).

Place the mushroom caps on an oiled baking sheet and fill with the mushroom mixture. Spoon some sauce over each one and sprinkle with the remaining cheese. Cook under the grill until well browned and bubbling.

At the same time, toast the bread under the grill, and cut it to the same size as the mushrooms. Place a mushroom on each piece of toast and serve at once.

pastry cream

Makes about
210 g/7½ oz

150 ml/5 fl oz/⅔ cup milk

¼ vanilla pod (vanilla bean), split
and seeds scraped out

1 egg yolk

20 g/scant ¼ oz/2 tbsp caster sugar
(US granulated sugar)

20 g/scant ¼ oz/2½ tbsp plain flour
(all-purpose flour), sifted

Put the milk, vanilla pod and seeds
in a pan and bring to the boil over a
gentle heat. In a bowl, whisk the egg
yolk and sugar together until pale
and creamy. Add the flour and mix
to a smooth paste. Pour on half of
the boiling milk and mix well. Return
the mixture to the pan with the
remaining milk, stirring to mix
well, and boil for 1 minute until
thickened, stirring constantly.
Pass through a fine sieve.

This will keep in the fridge for 2–3
days. If you make it in advance, be
sure to chill it quickly and
thoroughly.

frangipane

Makes about
425 g/15 oz

120 g/4 oz/8 tbsp unsalted butter, at room temperature

120 g/4 oz/½ cup + 2 tbsp caster sugar (US granulated sugar)

2 eggs, beaten

25 g/¾ oz/3 tbsp plain flour (all-purpose flour), sifted

120 g/4 oz/1⅔ cups ground almonds, sifted

Cream the butter with the sugar using an electric mixer until light and fluffy. Slowly add the eggs, with the machine running. Add the flour and almonds and mix together well. Keep, covered, in the refrigerator

choux pastry

Makes about
280 g/10 oz

120 ml/4 fl oz/½ cup milk

50 g/2 oz/4 tbsp unsalted butter

65 g/2½ oz/7½ tbsp plain flour (all-purpose flour), sifted

pinch of salt

2 eggs

Put the milk and butter in a saucepan and bring to the boil until the butter has melted. Reduce the heat, add the flour and salt, and stir well until the mixture forms a smooth paste. Cook, stirring, for 2–3 minutes. Transfer to a bowl and beat in the eggs, one at a time. Use while still slightly warm.

puff pastry

675 g/1½ lb unsalted butter

675 g/1½ lb/4¼ cups plain flour
(all-purpose flour)

1–1½ tsp salt

275 ml/9½ fl oz/1 cup + 3 tbsp
water, chilled

juice of ½ lemon

Work together 500 g/1 lb 2 oz/1 lb
+ 4 tbsp of the butter with 175 g/
6 oz/1¼ cups of the flour on a cool
surface. When well mixed, form this
butter paste into a block and
refrigerate.

Rub the remaining butter into the
remaining flour with the salt until
the mixture resembles fine
breadcrumbs. Add the chilled water
and lemon juice to form a dough,
and mix until smooth and elastic.

Shape the dough into a ball, then
cut a cross in the top to one-third of
the depth. Open out the points of
the cross and roll out each one to a

flap about 5 mm/¼ inch thick,
12.5 cm/5 inches wide and 12.5
cm/5 inches long. Place the butter
paste in the centre of the dough and
fold the flaps over, folding
anticlockwise and ensuring that the
edges are well sealed.

Roll out the dough into a 30 x 60
cm/12 x 24 inch rectangle. Fold the
short sides to meet in the middle,
then fold in half like a book to form
four equal layers; this is called a
double-turn. Cover with a damp
cloth and leave to rest in the
refrigerator for at least 30 minutes.

Repeat to give the dough four more
double-turns, resting in the
refrigerator each time, then leave the
dough, covered, in the refrigerator to
rest, preferably overnight, before
using.

sweet pastry

Makes about
700 g/1 lb 9 oz

225 g/8 oz/1 cup unsalted butter

100 g/4 oz/½ cup caster sugar
(US granulated sugar)

1 egg, beaten

350 g/12 oz/3 cups plain flour
(all-purpose flour)

salt

Cream the butter and sugar together until very pale. Slowly beat in the egg. Slowly add the flour with a pinch of salt and mix to a smooth paste.

Cover and leave to rest in the refrigerator for at least 1 hour before using.

sugar syrup

Makes about
600 ml/1 pint/
2½ cups

250 g/8½ oz/1¼ cups caster sugar
(US granulated sugar)

500 ml/16 fl oz/2 cups water

a few drops of lemon juice

Put the sugar and water in a saucepan and dissolve over a gentle heat, swirling occasionally. Add the lemon juice and bring to the boil. Boil for 1 minute and then leave to cool. The syrup will keep in the refrigerator for 1–2 weeks.